Ill-Gotten Gold

Quotes

"I believe we're all temporarily insane from 15-25. That doesn't excuse our behavior, at those ages, but it does help explain it...."

"'Wait,' I said. 'So, would you two get knighted while I got hung for this?' They didn't answer; they just laughed and turned their smiling, youthful faces towards me...."

Ill-Gotten Gold

Looking like a *buxom wench*, my niece Bonnie's ample bosom was as laced up, spilling over, and tortured as the *best* of them. Her beefy, bearded fiancé Buck wore a brown tunic and tights over *rather-nice* gams. They'd just come from the jousting tournament and festival of an international society recreating medieval European culture.

Making a meal of the massive turkey legs and sweet mead they'd brought from the fest, the three of us sat out, by a big fire, on a cool, spring evening in the West Virginia Mountains. The fire smoke kept away the bugs, common along the Potomac River.

"I ran into that society years ago," I told them, disturbing the dust covering my forgotten memory.

"Did you have a good time?" Bonnie asked. Firelight danced across her impressive bust line, her cheeks, and her bright, young eyes.

"Ah, no. Can't say I did. Geez. I haven't thought about this in *years*. The more I *think* about it, the more I'd just as soon *change the subject.*"

"*Why?*" Buck asked. "What happened?"

I hesitated. Then, I asked, "would you two like to hear an old-fashioned confession I should probably make before I die?" Buck nodded. He shrugged a bit, as if to say, "why not?"

Bonnie said, "have at it." So, I did.

I told them, "on the first morning of spring break, decades ago, I headed out of the Pitt dorms with two of my five suite mates. In our back pockets, each of us carried a flask of bourbon, leftover from our party the night before.

We made a meal of massive turkey legs and sweet mead.

"One of the two, a regional rugby player from a large family of boys, went along to stretch her legs, as did I. The other, an art student from the Pittsburgh suburbs, needed to catch the last day of a museum exhibit, which was the reason for our trip. I don't even remember what exhibit we saw, but it was a few miles up the road, near Schenley Park.

"Afterwards, we walked towards the park's woods, for a stroll along the shady trails on a sunny day.

"Gathered in the field, near some entrances to the woods, we found a group of men and a few horses, all dressed in metal mesh and other armor. My Pittsburgh roommate smiled, waved, and spoke up cheerfully in the local slang, asking them, *'What'r youns* **doin'***?'*

"The men spoke over each other with pride and excitement about a 'quest for gold, hidden in the park.'

"'As soon as a few more knights arrive,' one burly man said, 'we'll be off.' They and their mounts shifted on their feet, itching to get started.

"In the spirit of the game, I smiled at them and asked, 'pray, ye knights, may we pass?' They seemed hesitant, seemed to be sizing us up.

"Our rugby player, who threatened college guys because she enjoyed wrestling with them, surprised me with a shockingly vacant, empty-headed stare into space. She hung back, a bit, and avoided engaging these grown men. This seemed odd but wise. Our pretty, Pittsburgh roommate giggled, twirled a curl of her hair. The tallest and best-costumed knight, who appeared to be their leader, gave us a smile.

"'*Ye may*,' he replied, stepping aside with a gracious sweep of his gloved hand towards the entrances to the wooded paths. The other knights parted, so that we might continue on our way."

He stepped aside with a gracious sweep of his gloved hand towards the wooded paths.

Bonnie and Buck watched me almost *too* intently. Each nodded, here and there, as I spoke.

They bit from the tasty turkey legs. They washed bites down with the mead, which was a bit sweet for my taste.

They were *so quiet*, I suspected the *mead* was working on them.

"And," Bonnie prompted, "what happened?"

"Well," I said, "my roommates and I had never heard of their society, but we wished the knights 'godspeed on thy quest,' or something like that, before we followed the path, to the right, into the woods.

"We strolled along the cool, dirt trail. We nipped on our flasks some more, smelled the fresh ferns, talked about a band playing that night, and we laughed about running into *armored knights*.

"As we walked deeper into the forest, we noticed little green and orange flags stuck in the ground, here and there, off into the trees. I watched the flags carefully. Once we passed the next bend, the pattern in the colors was clear.

"'This pattern's so obvious,' I said. 'What they're searching for is over at that yellow flag.'

"We hiked in to the flag. There, on the ground, just behind the edge of a boulder, sat a rock, about a foot by a foot, flat on the bottom, rounded on the top, and painted bright, sparkling gold.

There, on the ground, sat the bright, sparkling gold.

"'*Oh my God! It's the gold!*' our rugby-player said. We all laughed out loud. I remember feeling pleased with myself for figuring out the location. 'We should *claim* it!' she insisted, in her typically competitive way.

"The other nodded. 'Let's *liberate* it,' she said, raising her flask in a toast before she drank. She was all for it, too.

"So susceptible to suggestion, then, was I, that that's *all* it took. I didn't think. I looked around, squatted down, covered the gold with my billowy hippie blouse, and scooped it up underneath.

"The three of us *roared* with laughter as I stood and held the cold, heavy rock, concealed, under my big shirt. The damp, flat side flushed-up perfectly with my abdomen, half-protected from the cold stone by my jeans. We headed off with my arms wrapped around what looked like an advanced pregnancy."

"YOU *stole* that *gold?*" Buck erupted. I nodded shamefully.

"I'm not proud of it," I said. "I believe we're all temporarily insane from 15-25. That doesn't *excuse* our behavior, at those ages, but it does help *explain* it. So, you add the liquor, on top of misguided camaraderie among *temporarily insane* peers, and, well—*yes*. We *did* that. We *stole* their gold. I'm sorry for my role in it. And, *honestly*, it feels *good* to confess it."

"Well, okay," Buck said, "but you're *famous*, well, you're *in*famous!"

"Oh, no, Buck," I said, "I don't think that anybody cares about—"

"No!" Bonnie announced, "that missing *gold* is *legend!*"

"*Legend,*" I repeated, without believing it.

"People in the society have been trying to solve *'the mysterious disappearance of the Schenley Park Gold'* for *years*," Bonnie explained. I stared at their honest faces.

"*Really?*" I asked

"*Really.* Where *is* it?" Buck wanted to know.

"Where—is it?" I repeated.

"Can you *imagine*, Buck," Bonnie said, "if *WE turn in* the **missing Schenley Park Gold!**"

"Wait," I said. "So, would you two get *knighted* while I got *hung* for this?" They didn't answer; they just *laughed* and turned their smiling, youthful faces towards me.

"So," Buck persisted, "where IS it?"

"Well," I said, "the short answer is—I don't know."

"What? *Why!*" he demanded.

"Well, as I said, I carried it out of the woods. It was *heavy*, though, so we followed some deer paths through what seemed the shortest distance out. Eventually, and *still laughing* by the way, we found ourselves down hill and near the main road.

"From behind the tree line, we peeked up the hill at a growing crowd of knights gathering at the spot where we'd entered the woods. Big hand motions, visors up, looking around, one knight threw his big metal glove down as he yelled at the leader—they were pretty flustered.

"We'd stopped laughing. They seemed to know the gold was missing, and we had *no plan*.

"Rarely dull, my roommates dashed to the road. They stopped running at the sidewalk, where they began walking towards campus and away from the knights.

"Still carrying the gold under my shirt, I followed slowly. I took my time, figured we were less obvious if we were separated, anyway.

"One of the two peeked back at me from time to time. Neither behaved as if we'd been spotted. The sidewalk was peppered with a few, other pedestrians. I sped up to match their pace but avoided their eye contact.

My arms ached. I took some even breaths, tried to stay calm, and resisted looking back towards the knights. I didn't want to draw their attention. Regardless, though, I knew I couldn't move *any faster*, even if they *were* on my tail.

"As I closed in on my roommates, I was searching for a place to ditch the gold. I couldn't carry it much longer and knew neither one of them was dressed to conceal it. I saw no cabs or buses around. At that moment, both of them stuck out a thumb. A little two-door stopped in a heartbeat.

"We crammed in, in a hurry—the two of them folded into the back with me last in, in the front. I held the gold in place, under my shirt, but in my lap, so my arms got a break from the weight. Calmly, I asked the balding driver if he'd, 'please drop us down the road at the Pitt dorms.'

"He turned his rubbery, furrowed face to me. Then, I saw his nearly, black-colored eyes in red-veined eyeballs, protruding about an inch farther out of his skull than normal. One eye was wonky. His mouth formed a weird, shady smirk below his wild, freaky, about-to-pop eyes. *All kinds* of shit was *wrong* with *this guy*.

"As he pulled back into traffic, I felt uneasy about his high creep factor, his high rate of speed, and where we were headed with this *spooky dude*.

He turned his rubbery, furrowed face to me.

"A pinch on the back of my arm led me to look back to my roommates. They parted and pointed to a couple dozen sets of mounted, human teeth, scattered on the shelf behind them. Bits of food seemed *stuck* in the teeth, and I smelled a rotten *stench* in the car.

"I saw their *wide* eyes fix on the front windshield and followed their stares to find *all* our eyes meeting *his*, *watching* us, in the rear-view mirror. His smirk intensified. He never *spoke* to us, and I don't believe he had any *teeth* in his mouth.

"The three of us were *freaking out*. Our rugby player leaned towards the driver and put on that blank stare. I couldn't decide if she were simply distancing herself from the teeth or plotting to lock him in some kind of wrestling hold. *Not good*. *Anything* could happen after that.

"I figured she knew how to cut off his air. Under the pressure, I pictured those pop eyes flying right out of his head as he passed out. I tried to meet her vacant eyes, shook my head, *hoped* she didn't move on him while he was driving. If she did, I'd have to grab the wheel while *he* controlled our speed.

"I rolled down the window, releasing some of the stench and tension. I figured I could open the door at the first stoplight. If I had to, I could make a scene big enough to stop traffic while we got out. If he tried anything, I'd pitch the rock on him, maybe throw it into the windshield—let him feast his wonky pop eyes on *that*.

"I was ready for anything.

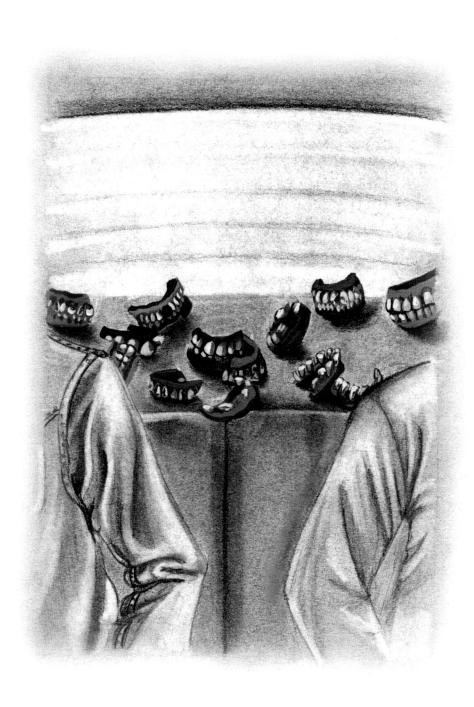

They parted and pointed to a couple dozen sets of mounted, human teeth.

"The green lights continued until we were nearly there. The car had barely stopped beneath the one, red light before the gold and I were out and the other two shot out on my heels—the first tumbled onto the crosswalk and the second landed on top of her.

"'Thanks for the lift,' I told him. I slammed the door with my foot, since I was still holding the rock, concealed under my shirt. My roommates untangled, helped each other up, and we we darted off the road before the light changed. I never looked back.

"Thrilled just to get *out* of *that* car, *that* marked the *first* and *last* time *I* hitched a ride."

"And, then?" Buck asked.

"And, then, well, that's it. Even after we *sobered up*, it never *occurred* to us to return the *gold*. Overall, the fear faded with time, and the adventure, which was *hilarious* to us for a while, became less remembered as life moved on."

"What happened to the **gold**?" Bonnie asked.

"Oh, right. We used it as a *doorstop* to our suite, for the rest of the year. We were too young and callous to feel shame for treating *chivalrous* knights with *dishonesty* and *thievery*. To *us*, the gold was a *fun conversation piece*. We used to say we'd, 'won it in a treasure hunt, against a bunch of guys, out in the woods,' which *was* mostly true.

"Soon, we began to overlook the doorstop. When we moved out, we left it there, holding the door open for the housekeeping crew."

"It *could* be there *still*," Buck said.

"I suppose it's possible. It *did* make a *good* doorstop—Brackenridge Hall, 4th floor, 1983."

"It's a *lead*," Buck said, smiling.

"It's a *worthy* quest!" Bonnie said with a grin. "We should take this intelligence to the society. Maybe they'll form an alliance with the *Pittsburgh* chapter to—"

"*Hey,*" I said, "if you two can do something *good* with *this* information, *that's great.* Just, *please, leave my name out of it, okay?* I don't come out looking so great in this sordid tale of ill-gotten gold." They nodded.

∈nd

(Please note: Some names and details may be altered or omitted to protect privacy, except mine.)

About the Story and the Series

"Ill-Gotten Gold," like the other Mostly-True Stories in the series, is mostly true. I call them "Mostly-True Stories" because—none of us is objective; because the weaving of any story includes subjective choices made in the crafting of it; and, because some names and details may be altered or omitted to protect privacy.

Meaty and accessible, these short stories are full of the kinds of tales someone might tell around a campfire. These Mostly-True Stories aim to help us enjoy taking a look at ourselves and our motivations. They also aim to leave a good wave in their wake. In an effort to reveal honorable truths, the stories weave—scary bits, funny bits, missing bits best left unsaid, the bits you can't make up or leave out, the touching bits that ring so true, connecting and summary bits, arresting moral bits, bits of lore, and more. *Mostly*, though, these stories ARE true.

In *"The Great Aunt Alice Collection,"* first in the series, a young girl navigates tall tales and telling truths told in rural Elk County, PA, from the 1870s to the 1970s. In the end, she finds herself protecting what she once feared, including the "Indians in the attic."

In the case of *"Ill-Gotten Gold,"* some temporarily insane, young adults catch Gold Fever, in Pittsburgh, and stumble their way through the consequences.

In *"The White Devil & the Twisted, Young Owl,"* three, old friends find adventure, humor, and hope while trying to save a twisted owl in D.C.-area woodlands.

I hope you enjoy these stories. If so, you may also like the Local-Character Blogs on www.megansdesk.net—one is "*Heartbreak Alley: Sausage Smoking & the Back-Woods Belly Dancing of Tullah Hanley*" and another is "*A Pleasant Fish Tale.*"

Thank you for your interest.

Out here,
Megan

About the Author

Author Megan Schreiber-Carter is a third-generation native of a storied, old borough in the Pennsylvania Wilds' Allegheny Mountains. For decades, she lived and worked along the Potomac River, in D.C.. These days, she finds more inspiration in the forests of her "native altitude," in the place her family's called "home" for more than 100 years. She creates award-winning, multi-media content for clients and audiences, worldwide. She values loved ones, honest conversation, mountain air, the woods, a good story, cooking time, clarity, natural remedies, preserving historic structures, a good dog, simplicity, peace, and sitting by the fire. More of her work may be found at: www.megansdesk.net.

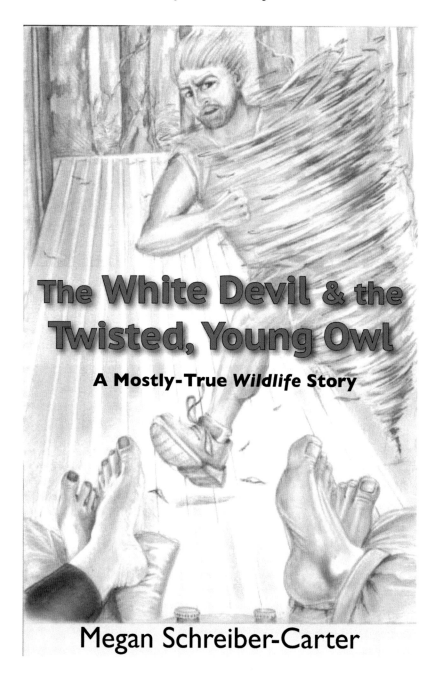

The White Devil & the Twisted, Young Owl

A Mostly-True *Wildlife* Story

Megan Schreiber-Carter

Many miles of woods grow inside the D.C. beltway. The forest here, along the Potomac River, is home to a variety of wildlife, including the humans—

"**We call Erik the 'White Devil' not because he's a *bad* guy, not *really*,** but because an elderly lady semi-affectionately dubbed him with the title. It fit, all too well, not only his very-white appearance but also his sometimes-questionable morality and his devilish tendency to laugh, without regard, at human failings others do **NOT** find funny. He's even been known to tempt others' vices—taking pastries to fat people, cigarettes to smokers, insults to the irritable, hard liquor to heavy drinkers…. Some quirk in Erik compelled him to find sport in the weaknesses of others…."

But, this situation with the Twisted, Young Owl was different—

The White Devil & the Twisted, Young Owl is the second short story in Megan's Mostly-True Stories series. (The first short story is **The Great Aunt Alice Collection**.)

Author **Megan Schreiber-Carter** is a third-generation native of the Pennsylvania Wilds' Allegheny Mountains and a career writer. Her bio and more of her writing may be found at **www.megansdesk.net.**

$14.99
ISBN 978-1-951448-03-5

Another Mostly-True Story in the Series

The Great Aunt Alice Collection
A Memoir and Mostly-True Story

Megan Schreiber-Carter

Wild souls, free spirits, and savage thoughts live on in the remarkable attic of a young girl growing up in the mountainous Pennsylvania Wilds, during the 1960s and 70s, among the grand, historic remains of a turn-of-the-1900s Boomtown.

"When my Aunt Alice was a teenager," Mom said, "she hopped on the train with her boyfriend, headed to New York City, with the intention of getting married. Her mother, your Great-Grandmother Lulu Muldoon, was on the next train and determined to stop them, which she would have, but she lost them in the New York train station...."

The Great Aunt Alice Collection presents tall tales and telling truths told in rural, Elk County, PA, from the late 1870s to the late 1970s, and hands out "pearls of wisdom from the living, breathing, soul-filled past."

"I looked for the Ghosts of the Forest, when we ice skated on the frog pond in the deep woods, but never saw them. 'Those will come alive in the spring, when it thaws,' Dad told us about the frogs—clearly frozen, mid-sprawl, in the ice under our feet. Now, who could believe that? Those frogs were certainly dead. This frog tale was just like the yellow-brown salve Dad put on our cuts—'Mrs. McKinley's bear salve.' Really? From a bear?...."

"If you want to understand today, you have to search yesterday." Pearl S. Buck

Author Megan Schreiber-Carter is a third-generation native of Pennsylvania's Allegheny Mountains and a career writer. Her bio and more of her writing may be found at www.megansdesk.net.

$14.99
ISBN 978-1-951448-02-8
51499

9 781951 448028

Local-Character Blogs at megansdesk.net

MEGAN'S DESK

Home   Web-Logs (Blogs)   A Retropolitan Borough (Photo Feature)   Mostly-True Short Stories   For Sale: Vintage   About Megan

Megan Schreiber-Carter ☕
May 2, 2021 · 2 min

Heartbreak Alley: Sausage Smoking & the Back-Woods Belly Dancing of Tullah...

Heartbreak Alley is a kick-back place in a rural-Pennsylvania, mountain borough. In good weather, garage bays are opened wide to the...

485 views   0 comments   5 ♡

Megan Schreiber-Carter ☕
Apr 30, 2020 · 3 min

A Pleasant Fish Tale

Fish for dinner, on Friday, is common in Elk County, PA, regardless of the time of year. At dinnertime one Friday, about a month and a...

674 views   0 comments   7 ♡

"Ill-Gotten Gold" Credits and Details

Illustrations: Erin McChesney
Layout: Sarah Rossey
Copyright: © 2022 Megan Schreiber-Carter
All rights reserved.
www.megansdesk.net
megan.schreiber@earthlink.net
https://www.facebook.com/Megan.Schreiber.Carter
Amazon Author's page: https://www.amazon.com/Megan-Schreiber-Carter/e/B08524RLG1?ref=sr_ntt_srch_lnk_1&qid=1647263849&sr=8-1
ISBN 978-1-951448-06-6 E-book
ISBN 978-1-951448-05-9 Paperback

Made in the USA
Middletown, DE
02 February 2023